How to Play FIFA

Score Your Way to Victory

Master the Skills and Tactics of Soccer Simulation

JADWIGA JOVITA

Table of Contents

CHAPTER ONE 6

   Introduction 6

   Understanding The Fifa Game 6

   Basic Controls And Navigation 7

   Getting Started: Establishing Your Team 8

   Mastering Passing And Ball Control 9

   Shooting Techniques: Achieving Goals With Precision..9

   Defensive Strategy: Keeping Your Opponents At Bay...10

CHAPTER TWO 13

   Advanced Tactics: Creating Opportunities And Capitalizing On Them............................13

   Understanding Players' Attributes And Formations...14

   Increasing Your Football IQ: Reading The Game..15

   Training Regimen: Improving Skills And Fitness..16

   Unlocking Special Moves And Tricks............18

   Building Your Ultimate Team: Players, Strategies, And Chemistry............................19

CHAPTER THREE 22
Chemistry And Squad Building 22
Chemical Dynamics 22
Squad Building Strategies 24
Navigating Career Mode: From Rookie To Legend 25
Starting 25
Player Development 26
Manage Your Club: Transfers, Contracts, And Finances 26
Transfer Market 27
Contract Negotiations 28

CHAPTER FOUR 29
Financial Management 29
Scouting Talent: Finding The Next Superstar 29
Scouting Network 30
Youth Development 30
Tactical Analysis: Breaking Down Opponents 31
Opponent Analysis 31
Tactical Flexibility 32

Online Play: Competing Against Global Players 32

CHAPTER FIVE 33

Online Seasons 33

Ultimate Teams 33

Playing In Tournaments And Leagues 34

FIFA World Cup 34

Online Leagues 35

Staying Current: Dlcs, Updates, And Patches 35

DLCs 35

Updates And Patches: 36

Troubleshooting: Common Problems And Solutions 36

Common Issues: 37

Fixes And Workarounds 37

CHAPTER SIX 39

Improving Gameplay: Customisations & Mods 39

Community And Social Integration 40

Fifa Evolution: A Brief History 41

Behind The Scenes: Development Insights .. 41

Future Of FIFA: Innovations And Expectations 42

Ethical Gaming Involves Fair Play And Sportsmanship 43

Conclusion..44

CHAPTER ONE

Introduction

Few virtual sports franchises have the clout and worldwide popularity of the FIFA series. FIFA, developed by Electronic Arts, has been a gaming staple since its release in 1993.

It has grown over time into a thorough simulation of the beautiful game, capturing the spirit of football and giving an immersive gaming experience to millions of gamers across the globe.

Understanding The Fifa Game

At its heart, FIFA is a football simulation game that attempts to capture the thrill and drama of live football matches. FIFA attempts to capture every facet of the sport, from the clamor of the audience to the complex strategies used by elite teams. Players may manage their favorite teams and players while playing in a variety of leagues, tournaments, and game types.

Basic Controls And Navigation

To navigate the virtual field in FIFA, you must learn the game's fundamental controls. Understanding the mechanics of passing, shooting, and guarding is essential while playing on a console or PC.

The controls are intended to be intuitive, enabling players to perform precise motions and activities with ease. With practice, players may improve their abilities and perform complicated maneuvers with ease.

Getting Started: Establishing Your Team

Before getting started, make sure your squad is set up according to your preferences and playing style. FIFA has a multitude of customization possibilities, enabling players to change formations, personnel, and tactics to fit their plans.

Whether you prefer a high-pressing offensive strategy or a more cautious defensive philosophy, customizing your squad is critical to success on the virtual field.

Mastering Passing And Ball Control

Passing and ball control are important abilities in FIFA, directing the flow of play and allowing for elaborate build-up sequences.

Understanding pass timing and trajectory, as well as using skill movements to dodge opponents, may open up scoring possibilities and break down obstinate defenses. Mastering these parts of the game takes practice and elegance, but the results are well worth the effort.

Shooting Techniques: Achieving Goals With Precision

The ultimate aim of FIFA is to score goals, which involves both talent and accuracy. From long-range screamers to delicate chip shots, there are several ways to send the ball to the back of the goal.

Understanding shooting mechanics, including shot strength, accuracy, and finesse, is critical for turning opportunities into goals. Whether you want to blast it past the keeper or finesse it into the corner, trying out new shooting styles will help you improve your game.

Defensive Strategy: Keeping Your Opponents At Bay

While offensive ability is important, effective defensive play is key in FIFA. Effective defensive techniques, such as pushing high up the pitch or sitting deep to absorb pressure, may frustrate and break opponents' rhythm. Timing tackles, interceptions and defensive posture are all essential components of a successful defensive strategy.

By being disciplined and organized at the back, you can negate the opposition's threats and offer your side the best opportunity of winning.

Finally, FIFA provides a comprehensive and engaging gaming experience that captures the spirit of football in ways never seen before. From learning fundamental controls to executing complex strategies, there is always something new to learn and discover in the world of

FIFA. Whether you're a seasoned veteran or a beginner to the game, the pleasure of scoring goals and battling against friends and opponents is what makes FIFA so unique.

So grab your controller, put on your virtual boots, and prepare to enjoy the stunning game in all its digital grandeur.

CHAPTER TWO

Advanced Tactics: Creating Opportunities And Capitalizing On Them

In the fast-paced world of football, knowing advanced tactics is critical for generating and capitalizing on chances. Understanding player traits and formations, as well as building your football IQ, are all critical to on-field success.

Additionally, concentrating on training regimens, unlocking special moves, and assembling your ideal squad will improve your talents and strategic prowess.

Understanding Players' Attributes And Formations

Player qualities and formations are critical components of football strategy. Each member contributes distinct talents and qualities to the squad, which must be recognized and used successfully.

Recognizing these characteristics, whether they be speed, agility, strength, or tactical intelligence, enables coaches and players to build methods that are suited to their specific strengths.

Formations influence team relationships and tactics on the pitch. Whether it's the traditional 4-4-2, the more contemporary 4-3-3, or variants like the 3-5-2, each configuration has advantages and disadvantages. Understanding how formations affect player placement, movement, and overall team structure is critical for carrying out game plans successfully.

Increasing Your Football IQ: Reading The Game

Developing a high football IQ is critical for success at all levels of the game. It entails comprehending the flow of the game, predicting opponents' actions, and making split-second judgments under pressure.

A strong football IQ enables players to understand the game, see trends, and exploit flaws in the opposing defense.

To improve your football IQ, you must study the game both on and off the pitch. Analyzing game tape, researching tactics, and learning from experienced players and coaches may all help improve your soccer intelligence.

Furthermore, regularly participating in game situations via drills, scrimmages, and simulations helps to build intuition and decision-making skills in real-world events.

Training Regimen: Improving Skills And Fitness

A complete training routine is necessary for increasing football abilities and fitness levels. Passing, dribbling, shooting, and defending are technical skills that must be mastered via constant practice. Furthermore, improving physical characteristics like as speed, endurance, strength, and agility is critical for sustaining optimum performance throughout the season.

Training sessions should be designed to focus on particular areas for growth while also including components of game-like settings. Drills that imitate match settings assist players in adapting their abilities to real-game scenarios.

Furthermore, adding strength and conditioning workouts designed for soccer-specific motions improves overall fitness and lowers the chance of injuries.

Unlocking Special Moves And Tricks

In football, learning specific maneuvers and tricks may provide players a huge edge on the pitch. Whether it's a step-over, a nutmeg, or a knuckleball free-kick, these moves may catch opponents off guard and provide scoring chances. However, perfecting these maneuvers demands serious effort and repetition to perform them consistently under duress.

Players may master specific maneuvers and tricks by combining independent practice with coaching guidance. Breaking down the mechanics of each technique and concentrating on understanding the basics is critical for success. Furthermore, implementing these techniques into game-like scenarios during training helps players develop confidence and execution under pressure.

Building Your Ultimate Team: Players, Strategies, And Chemistry

Building the best team takes more than just individual brilliance; it also demands cohesiveness, chemistry, and tactical knowledge. It is critical to choose athletes who not only have the requisite talents but also balance each other's strengths and shortcomings. Furthermore, developing tactical methods that maximize the team's talent and playing style is critical to success on the pitch.

Developing team chemistry entails cultivating a good team culture, communication, and trust among players. Team-building events, group conversations, and common objectives all contribute to increased bonding and cohesiveness both on and off the pitch.

Furthermore, recognizing each player's position on the team and how they contribute to the team's overall performance is critical for developing a cohesive and successful unit.

To summarise, learning advanced tactics in soccer is a complicated process that includes understanding player traits, and formations, increasing soccer IQ, adopting a tough training program, unlocking unique moves, and forming a cohesive squad.

By concentrating on these characteristics, players and coaches may generate and capitalize on possibilities for on-field success.

CHAPTER THREE

Chemistry And Squad Building

In the realm of virtual football, chemistry, and squad building are critical components that may determine a team's success. Understanding how chemistry works and mastering the art of creating a cohesive team are essential skills for any prospective manager aiming to dominate the digital field.

Chemical Dynamics

Chemistry in virtual football refers to the cohesiveness and synergy between players on the field. It is not enough to have a group of top players; it is also important to know how effectively they operate together as a team. A variety of elements impact chemistry, including player positions, nationality, league affiliation, and club ties.

Each player has a chemistry rating, and the team's overall chemistry is calculated as a weighted average of the individual players' chemistry ratings.

Building chemistry entails picking players whose characteristics complement one another and who have strong links, whether via a similar country, participation in the same league, or affiliation with the same club.

Squad Building Strategies

Building a successful team requires a planned strategy. Managers must pick players based on their chosen formation, play style, and financial restraints.

A balanced team usually consists of offensive stars, midfield maestros, competent defenders, and a dependable custodian.

Furthermore, managers must consider players' roles and duties within the squad. This involves choosing captains, set-piece takers, and the leadership structure. A well-structured squad not only improves performance on the field but also promotes team spirit and togetherness.

Navigating Career Mode: From Rookie To Legend

Career Mode allows players to take on the role of a football manager and lead their favorite team to victory. Whether beginning at the bottom of the league ladder or leading a top-tier squad, the path from rookie to legend is laden with trials and victories.

Starting

Starting a career mode for the first time might be intimidating. It is critical to choose the proper club that corresponds with your management goals and objectives. Every career mode experience is unique, whether it's bringing a legendary club back to its former glory or leading a little squad on a fairy tale path to the top.

Player Development

One of the most important features of career mode is player growth. Managers are responsible for developing young talent, identifying potential possibilities, and grooming them into world-class superstars. Balancing player training, match experience, and relaxation is critical for unlocking individual potential and preserving team unity.

Manage Your Club: Transfers, Contracts, And Finances

Managing a football club entails more than simply tactics and player selection; it also requires careful financial planning and smart transfer negotiations. From negotiating player contracts to balancing the finances, good club management is critical to long-term success.

Transfer Market

The transfer market allows managers to enhance their squads by purchasing and selling players. Scouting talent, recognizing development opportunities, and negotiating agreements under budget limits are all essential components of successful transfer market navigation.

Shrewd additions may catapult a squad to victory, whilst disastrous moves can put a club back for seasons.

Contract Negotiations

Managing player contracts requires a careful balancing act. Managers must arrange contracts that meet both the players and the club's financial requirements. Salary, contract terms, release conditions, and performance incentives are all important factors to consider.

Retaining important players and avoiding contract conflicts is critical for team stability and motivation.

CHAPTER FOUR

Financial Management

Balancing the club's finances is an important part of management. Managers must carefully distribute finances, balancing player pay, transfer fees, and operating costs. Revenue generation via ticket sales, merchandising, and sponsorship partnerships is critical for the team's financial stability and long-term success.

Scouting Talent: Finding The Next Superstar

Scouting talent is a critical component in team construction. Effective scouting, whether unearthing undiscovered gems or acquiring known stars, may provide a team with a competitive advantage.

Scouting Network

Establishing a strong scouting network is critical for spotting talent throughout the world. Managers may send out scouts to look for players based on certain criteria like age, position, and potential. Scouting reports give essential information on a player's abilities, potential, and appropriateness for the squad.

Youth Development

Investing in youth development may provide long-term advantages to the team. Managers may foster young talent via the club's academy system, allowing them to improve their abilities and ultimately break into the main squad. Developing homegrown talent enriches the team while also instilling a feeling of pride and identity in the club.

Tactical Analysis: Breaking Down Opponents

Tactical analysis is critical to getting a competitive edge in the virtual field. Managers may develop efficient plans and adjust their tactics by analyzing their opponents' strengths and shortcomings.

Opponent Analysis

Analyzing opponents includes examining their playing style, formations, and important players. Managers may utilize in-game data and match replays to detect trends and tendencies, enabling them to predict their opponents' movements and exploit weaknesses.

Tactical Flexibility

Adapting strategies in the middle of the game is critical to victory. Managers must be proactive in reacting to the ebb and flow of the game, whether it means making replacements, changing formation, or adjusting playing instructions. Tactical flexibility may change the course of a game and earn crucial victories.

Online Play: Competing Against Global Players

For those looking for the ultimate challenge, online gaming allows you to compete against gamers from all around the globe.

CHAPTER FIVE

Online Seasons

Online seasons enable users to engage in a series of matches against opponents with comparable skill levels. Climbing the ranks and being promoted takes talent, tenacity, and flexibility. Whether you're competing for bragging rights or striving for the top division, online seasons provide a competitive and fulfilling environment.

Ultimate Teams

Ultimate Team is a popular online game in which users may create their ideal team by acquiring player cards via packs or trade. The key to Ultimate Squad's success is to build camaraderie and assemble a powerful squad. Competing in online tournaments and leagues enables individuals to demonstrate their abilities while earning incentives.

Playing In Tournaments And Leagues

Participating in tournaments and leagues is an exciting experience that enables players to compete against the finest in the world.

FIFA World Cup

The FIFA World Cup is the pinnacle of international football, and many players dream of playing in the virtual competition. Representing your nation on a worldwide scale and vying for greatness is a once-in-a-lifetime opportunity.

Online Leagues

Joining an online league enables gamers to engage in organized tournaments against other players. Whether it's a casual league with friends or a serious league with competent opponents, the excitement of battling for the crown is unparalleled.

Staying Current: Dlcs, Updates, And Patches

Staying current with the newest DLCs, updates, and patches is critical for having the greatest gameplay experience possible.

DLCs

Downloadable content (DLC) provides new features, modes, and material to the game, keeping it interesting and engaging for gamers. DLCs, whether in the form of new stadiums, player faces, or game modes, improve the gaming experience and offer value for users.

Updates And Patches:

Regular updates and patches fix bugs, malfunctions, and gameplay difficulties, resulting in a smooth and pleasurable gaming experience. Staying up to speed on the latest updates and patches is critical for optimum performance and gameplay balance.

Troubleshooting: Common Problems And Solutions

Despite the greatest efforts of developers, users may run across typical bugs and errors when playing.

Knowing how to fix these difficulties might enable gamers to return to enjoying the game uninterrupted.

Common Issues:

Common difficulties include game crashes, network issues, and gameplay flaws. Identifying the fundamental cause of the problem is the first step towards a resolution.

Fixes And Workarounds

Developers often offer patches and updates to solve common problems and defects. In the interim, gamers may attempt troubleshooting measures including restarting the game, upgrading drivers, or altering in-game settings to temporarily fix the issue.

To summarise, mastering chemistry and squad building, navigating career mode, managing club finances, scouting talent, tactical analysis, online play, competing in tournaments and leagues, staying up to date on DLCs, updates, and patches, and troubleshooting common issues are all important aspects of the virtual football experience.

Understanding and mastering these ideas allows players to improve their game and lead their team to victory on the digital field.

CHAPTER SIX

Improving Gameplay: Customisations & Mods

In today's dynamic gaming environment, increasing gameplay via customizations and modifications has become an essential component of many gaming communities. These modifications, frequently produced by users or independent developers, provide unique chances to personalize and enhance gaming experiences.

Customizations and modifications, ranging from basic visual tweaks to major adjustments impacting gameplay mechanics, have revolutionized the gaming environment, including FIFA.

Community And Social Integration

The FIFA community thrives on social interaction, with players from all around the world gathering to exchange experiences, techniques, and, of course, modifications.

Online forums, social media groups, and specialized modding communities serve as gathering places for enthusiasts to interact, cooperate, and share ideas. This feeling of community promotes a dynamic ecology in which creativity thrives and discoveries arise regularly.

Fifa Evolution: A Brief History

Since its beginnings in 1993, the FIFA series has witnessed a tremendous transformation, moving from pixelated sprites to realistic simulations. With each version, the game has added innovative features, better visuals, and improved gaming mechanics. From the advent of career modes and Ultimate Team to the incorporation of motion capture technology, FIFA has continuously pushed the limits of what is possible in sports gaming.

Behind The Scenes: Development Insights

Behind FIFA's shiny veneer is a complicated network of development procedures that are methodically carried out by teams of designers, programmers, and artists.

From player ratings and stadium specifics to in-game physics and animations, every part of the game is meticulously scrutinized and refined. Development insights provide a window into the devotion and ingenuity that propels the franchise forward, showcasing the difficulties and successes encountered by the development team.

Future Of FIFA: Innovations And Expectations

As technology advances, the future of FIFA offers limitless opportunities for innovation. The potential for virtual reality integration and augmented reality experiences, as well as artificial intelligence-driven gaming upgrades, is vast.

Players look forward to each new update, excited to discover what breakthrough innovations and enhancements await them on the virtual field.

Ethical Gaming Involves Fair Play And Sportsmanship

Despite the fervor of competition, ethical gaming ideals remain central to the FIFA community. Fair play and sportsmanship serve as guiding principles, ensuring that games are played with honesty and respect. From following the game's rules to supporting tolerance and diversity, players respect a code of behavior that improves the gaming experience for everyone involved.

Conclusion

Finally, customizations and modifications play an important role in improving the FIFA gaming experience, increasing community participation, and pushing innovation within the series.

As the game evolves and adapts to evolving technology and player expectations, one thing is certain: the FIFA community's enthusiasm and inventiveness will continue to determine its future, ensuring that it stays a popular fixture in the world of sports gaming for years to come.

Made in the USA
Monee, IL
10 September 2024